TAPPING OUT

POEMS

NANDI COMER

TRIQUARTERLY BOOKS/NORTHWESTERN UNIVERSITY PRESS
EVANSTON, ILLINOIS

TriQuarterly Books
Northwestern University Press
www.nupress.northwestern.edu

Printed in the United States of America

10 9 8 7 6 5 4 3 2 1

Library of Congress Cataloging-in-Publication Data

Names: Comer, Nandi, author.
Title: Tapping out : poems / Nandi Comer.
Description: Evanston, Illinois : TriQuarterly Books/Northwestern
    University Press, 2020.
Identifiers: LCCN 2020000206 | ISBN 9780810142091 (paperback) |
    ISBN9780810142107 (ebook)
Subjects: LCSH: Lucha libre—Poetry. | Masks—Symbolic aspects—Poetry.
Classification: LCC PS3603.O4764 T37 2020 | DDC 811.6—dc23
LC record available at https://lccn.loc.gov/2020000206

For Menelik and for Pancho

Why should the world be over-wise,
In counting all our tears and sighs?
Nay, let them only see us, while
      We wear the mask.

—PAUL LAURENCE DUNBAR, *WE WEAR THE MASK*

When, beneath the black mask, a human being begins to make himself felt one cannot escape a certain awful wonder as to what kind of human being it is.

—JAMES BALDWIN, *STRANGER IN THE VILLAGE*

CONTENTS

ACKNOWLEDGMENTS

I am grateful to my colleagues, friends, and family for all the support and patience that made this publication possible: Mosco Aguilar, Terry Blackhawk, Maria Derás, Tarfia Faizullah, Perry Janes, Ceci Magaña, Toni Moceri, Denis Rochac, Sophia Softky, Ingrid Valencia, Miguel Valverde Castillo, and Ross White; to all of my students at Educaré: Escuela para el Éxito; to my professors and advisors at Indiana University: Catherine Bowman, Dr. Valerie Grim, Adrian Matejka, and the late Dr. Frederick McElroy; to my cohort and fellow classmates in the Creative Writing Program and the African American and African Diaspora Studies Department at Indiana University; to the institutions who gave me a space to write, including the Vermont Studio Center, the Virginia Center for the Creative Arts, Callaloo, and Cave Canem; to Parneshia Jones, Maia Rigas, and the staff at Northwestern University Press for their diligence, their sharp eyes, and their patience; to Ife-Chudeni for being the first eye; to Tommye Blount, Kahn Davison, Aricka Foreman, francine j. harris, Jamaal May, Matthew Olzmann, and Scheherazade Washington Parrish for your friendship and poet love; to Brenda Cárdenas for daring me to write this book; to Ross Gay and Vievee Francis for continuing to challenge me; to my sister, Shashu Harris, for my one and only fight; to Francisco "Pancho" Cardenas Rojas for introducing me to the only sport I've ever loved; and of course to Saeed and Menelik, thank you.

TAPPING OUT

ON BECOMING A FAN

Don't blame masks. Blame smoke.
Blame the tricky sorcery
of shiny boots, capes,
and props. Blame spandex's
tight grip on wrestlers' thighs.

When swollen biceps of masked men
slap canvas, how like broken toys
their bodies become, each one
proffering his limbs to the other.
And we, their spectators, hooked

under pain's smelly spell,
cannot resist wanting
sweat and blood. We rouse,
like tiny rioters, wave our fists,
curse the winner.

Blame the winning wrestler,
how he radiates,
center stage, how he performs
his own ascension up ropes,
his thick arms, hot and throbbing.

Blame his left foot poised
top turnbuckle. Blame
his hands-on-waist pose,
or the braying crowd,
or the thud his leg makes

as he falls, hacking down
on his opponent's
waiting chest.

Don't blame masks. Blame
spicy pork rinds and their vendors.

Blame bikini-clad women
with CORONA
and TECATE splayed
across their asses and tits.
Can boys be blamed for imitating

their fathers, leaning in,
praying his man clobbers
the other guy? I blame
a fourth-grade shoving match
with my sister.

My forehead turned hot
by an early June sun.
I hadn't understood
how anger, like a hot spring,
boils at the belly's core

until its hostile vapor
clenched my fists. I never tried
to weigh muscle against meat.
Never had to throw a punch.
I blame the thin hush

an audience becomes
as bone-tired men stumble
into their musty dressing rooms,
how their faces elude us
each match—the windswept dirt

under the feet of ten-year-old
onlookers, their cheering
for my sister's grip. Blame
the swirled marble buttons
of our school uniforms,

the impossibly long wait
for recess. Blame
the purple blooming bruise
sketched by the brushstroke
of her hands.

I have not thrown a punch since.
I wish I had bright sparkling
fabric hidden under
my dress shirt. Blame
the seams of a practiced persona

into which we've all
neatly wrapped our arms.
Blame the seamstress
who sewed this mask
and cut all the loose threads.

This arena is a site for unveiling,
my locale for loosening the strings.

LUCHA LIBRE

\loo'-chah· lee'-bray: 1. Wrestling 2. Mexican-style
wrestling known for its high-flying aerial power
moves and wrestlers that use masks to conceal
their identities. Also known as "all-in wrestling,"
"free wrestling," "the poor man's sport."

POSTCARDS, A SELF-PORTRAIT

*after Joseph Cornell, A Swan Lake for Tamara Toumanova
(Homage to the Romantic Ballet), 1946*

I am searching the merry-go-round of museum cards
a typewriter, a man holding his face in the night,

a white urinal. No. No. No. Dancers, frozen
on the side of a vase. Maybe? No.

The museum is far from home, so I look
for something my mother will like.

Dalí's pointed mustache stops my turning, his big eyes
roll out of his face like he is wanting to sneeze. I hold back

a tickle in my nose and push the carousel. I spot
Goya's gory giant. She does not like dark paintings.

She likes royal portraits. She likes masks.
She has never liked ballerinas. I stop

the revolving postcards. A blue shadow box,
a swan's neck bent into its back. Everything is blue.

Every tree and every cloud, every leaf, blue
and suspended by wire. I cannot.

I go to turn again, but the bird's beak won't let me.
So I pull the card from its place, lift it closer to my face.

I know she will not like it. She will think its figure strange.
Just as I think to return the swan, I see another face,

an African face, sticking out from the bottom of a pile.
The sketched lines of his torso unfinished and disappearing

near the borders. There is no blue.
No bird. I buy them both.

I woke with the word
on my tongue—*slap*—
unsure how to loosen
its stiff sound tacked
on my voice. *Slap.*
I tried mouthing
some other vowel,
some softer sound.
In the shower,
through breakfast,
all day—*slap*—
idled in my jaws.
Creeping under the brass
faucet's glint,
at the bottom of my china
cup, in the folds of taffeta
curtains—*slap*.

Then came the snippets:
a boy's anxious eyebrows
and surprised ovaled
lips; a worn armrest
under a black gloved hand.
At dinner, the kitchen girl
dribbled gravy
on my pulled chicken.
I thought blood,
and spit. I imagined
a whole body
working its weight
into a weapon.
I whispered *boot*.

In the metal bit
of my horse's mouth
I saw smoke, and tassels.
I said *mask*.
I held my tongue.

Back in my stable
the thin legs of a spider
scaling the wood wall
became fine fingers,
balled themselves
into a sweaty punch.
I said *blow*.

Tonight I scrub my tongue,
but the words unravel.
I lay them in my cheek,
suck down every single
syllable. I try to forget
all the heavy words.
Microphone. Spandex.
Each a tightly laced
note, a rubber sole
on my neck.

¡SANGRE! ¡SANGRE! ¡SANGRE!

No one knows if blood will come,
but once Terrible has a handful

of Místico's golden-rimmed eyehole
we are all on our feet, stirred up, chanting.

Center ring, both bulgy-bodied men
lift and fall in heavy, syncopated pants.

Every inch of Místico's body goes slack
from las patadas, los sentones,

and the choke out against ropes.
Each yank wrenches his masked head upward.

Under the weight of so much body,
threads give. This fight is about blood.

Bleeding a masked man starts
with a tiny rip, maybe a bite,

always broken skin. One cut
takes little pressure

to make a bloody spout. From countless bleedings,
heads callus. It is said some fighters

have been sliced so many times, temples
buckle into blankets of skin. Then

the leathered fortress
can only be sliced by a skilled blade.

Terrible breaks a hole in Místico's cloth crown.
The crowd's fists pump upward.

Each set of eyes opens in unison
with the tear. We want it.

We want to catch sight
of a damp hairline, a frowsy eyebrow,

then Místico's open skin.
What's so fascinating about watching

an opened temple? Why cheer
for a fighter pushing another man

to the brink of passing out?
Blood comes because we, the audience,

have asked for it. Before this match
the man in the third row, under howls

from his foreman, hauled emptied corn husks
through a second shift at an oil refinery.

The stench of burnt oil still sticks
to his dull frame. The young man next to him

is a waiter stretching his payday
between university books and his mother's

dinner table. Across the arena is a tired
sixth grade English teacher whose

semester is almost up. Here when we chant
Chair! Místico will shatter the wooden frame

across Terrible's back. When we yell for a flying
head scissors kick, Terrible is already lifting his boot.

Tonight we want blood.
We want to see arms and legs

fold and submit, to hear
the referee's three count.

If this were a street brawl,
planting ourselves curbside,

begging for the blade
would be beastly, but this

is an arena, and we are ready
to watch Terrible take his teeth

to Místico's skull. We lust
for the shaking arms, the loser's

flailing limbs. If any red beads
are to spot up, engorge,

and mix with a fighter's sweat,
we will have to yell for it again and again.

We want the trick, the whole bloody craft.
Místico's wound starts its spill.

We are on our feet. The slick words
grow fat on our tongues.

Rendered cloth and sparkle,
matching cape and boot.
When I am tacked to his face,
I am the winner. No small feature
framed without my lace-tightened grip
holding his role. The crowd
remembers how my studded mouth
curves around his lips, how I keep
my place despite the sweaty slipping
pull and fight. When he leaves the ring
he can take out another face,
he can go back to claiming
his uncloaked name.
Here, in this ring,
I am his camouflage,
his veil.

LOSING BETWEEN MANHOLES AND MYTHS

Here, girls keep ears tuned to heavy thunder,
rippled sky, and cloudbursts—not to boys' eyes
following hemlines, or catcalls from rooftops,
or a sweet shepherding palm at their waists.
It's the rains that dump women curbside,

wet and cored, never an unmarked taxi
or stumbling through our stone town's dark dawn.
October is a constant downpour.
Sidewalks overflow. Water whirlpools
at every corner. Red awnings drip

with their weight. The storms in this town
have already drowned many women.
If a girl is not careful she is pulled
underground through an uncovered manhole.
She won't fall into a ditch, or come back

with one broken limb. It's not the dragging
that swells their thin arms, not mouthfuls
of gravel, not their tongues snipped off
and jammed into mailboxes. A drizzle turns
to thrill then threat. Knuckles washed translucent

can't endure the pull. I know
what your newspapers say, but our men
don't turn their steering wheels down a dead-end street,
they don't stop in front of a house
she doesn't know. She will not need to kick

or scratch or plead that her father
is willing to pay ten times he asks
if she just makes it home. I'm telling you
every southwest corner does not lead
to a knot she can't loosen, nor

a stained cloth she can't spit up. Lower
your window. Breathe heavy humid air.
Fear streams of gutter water
rivering through the town. Flood rain takes
girls with muck and waste. The sewers make

them bloated. It's the storms that send
their bodies crawling through piping
towards a lake where all bobbing heads spring up.

DETROIT, LLORONA, MY HEART, MY CITY

Another ripped night, another dank song,
another bloated head of a headline child
bobs in your river. Loaded barrel woman,

pumped piston city, seven of your boys
rushed a townhouse door for jewelry,
for a cable box, for a game console,

tossed over kitchen tables, turned another boy's face
to mush. And you? You've gone and given up
their ghosts. Singing a murderous sinfonietta

you make another girl, another son dance
on the waves of your wails as if each bullet
were a small celebration missile. I know

this lost loveluck is not your fault. You do not mean
to change a father's body to canopy
and shield, into a dead weight your daughter

will tuck herself under until your singing
is done, but I've watched you strained with moan
and hymn. Your living room floor scattered

with obituaried flaking faces.
I've seen your organ arms' frantic wave. The length
of your fingers curved around carnation stems.

Each night your skin twists mourn to mourn. Beating
chest woman, yours is a solitary grief
whose wailing provokes the next hand hooked

to an infant throat. Weeping woman—
foolish mother. I've tried to sing your praise song,
but each of your river-drowned children

is a clanging cord in my throat. *Don't stay,*
you warn. You refuse to protect me.
Still, I drag myself to you, kneel and kiss

your oily asphalt knees. No one knows
your grieving songs, our love of graveyard strolls.
If only to fondle the fringes

of small caskets I come back. I retreat.
I come back. I retreat.

The American assassin, Denzel,
is cutting off a Mexican man's fingers
for stealing the blond child worth so much
in this movie. Denzel, the kidnappers,
the crooked cops—every body
is greasy with sweat or blood. My uncle
looks from the screen to me.
You live there? Are they really like that?
We are watching a rented film flash
statues and streets of a country
my uncle will never visit.
I am his world-wandering niece
visiting home from a dusty Tapatío town,
so I must have seen these bodies.
I have never seen the city
the camera flitters and cuts through,

but Denzel is already blowing it up. My uncle's
perched on the edge of his couch cushions,
balancing a dinner plate weighed down
by macaroni and cheese and corn bread.
He dips strands of turkey into oily
collard juice, and stares at Denzel,
with his Denzel pimp-limp stride,
turning over the city the way Denzel
turns over a city in a movie.
I mean, do they really kidnap people?

I mean, aren't you afraid they'll take you?
I cross lingual borders with other bodies
back and forth through cities
where there is no soul food and no blond girls
being taken from Denzel, and no Denzels
dying for the freedom of little blond girls.
There are towns where no one says kidnapping.

19

Denzel slips on slim sleek shades and tilts his head
toward an evaporating horizon. I don't want
to answer my uncle's questions.
I don't want to have to tell him
sometimes a gritty danger walks with my American
body, that I code my tongue in front of taxi drivers,
that I talk loud in cafés so everyone knows
I am fluent. Denzel keeps demanding,
La niña. La niña. ¿Donde está la niña?

I want to take my uncle's plump, brown wrist
and walk him through my neighborhood:
a tortillería, a hardware store, my lavandería,
the closest place for a torta—down the street,
a Walmart. I know he would stop
at a corner cart for a hot dog
wrapped in bacon and covered in cream.

I want to teach him the word *secuestro*
only means gone, and I am not a girl
that can be gone. I lie. I watch the pale child
run through the country of dogs and cumbia
towards Denzel. The smoldering metropolis
sprawls behind her. Denzel is already dead.
Gone. The kidnappers are already dead. Gone.
My uncle shrugs and digs his fork
into his plate and the little blond girl keeps running on.

ON COMING HOME TO TEACH

I tell my student he is not a corpse.
I know. I am a wrecked train. I show him

my scars. He holds up a hand, and peeks
back at me through a hole some boys stabbed

out of his palm. We've never seen each other
outside school, but we wake

on the same block to women damning a man's fists.
He sneaks into gated backyards with chained

pit bulls, sometimes hoping their angry collars
snap. I've known what it is to pacify panic.

Singing words are useless, cold water
splashed over sidewalk blood. When I leave

he will cut off his tongue, tame his outbursts.
Each day Death will bend his body into his desk.

If I speak for him, it will only return my fear.
If I speak for him, this poem is his suicide note.

ENMASCARADO, -A

\en-mas-cah-rah'-doh, -ah: 1. A masked wrestler.
2. A fighter who will risk everything to keep his/her
disguise. Once a fighter loses his/her mask, the
fighter loses his/her identity and possibly all rights
to enter the ring.

HOW NOT TO LOSE THE MASK: MIL MÁSCARAS SHOWERS AFTER A MATCH

Masked wrestlers will go pretty far to avoid being identified and seen without their masks by fan.—REY MYSTERIO

Through the locker room,
past the champion posters, past
the black and white TV monitor,
in the last shower stall,
Mil Máscaras feels
the weight of his arms
                              and sinks.
The tenderness of biceps, the pull
of hamstrings, each sore muscle
cooled by a cement bench.
While other fighters vacate
the locker room, he waits
for the shower to warm.
He loosens each tight loop
laced up his white boot,
wonders how many blows
his back has taken, how many
slaps across his chest. Still
ringside, clusters of boys grip
tattered autographs and wait
for a glimpse of eyebrow,
for the faintest ridge of nose.
Mil Máscaras slips each leg
out of spandex, cuts tape
from wrists.
There are times to leave
the embroidered *M* boxed
at home: movie theaters,
weddings, grocery shopping. One time
while a cashier dragged his cans

and bottles across a beeping scanner,
he studied her bored mouth,
how her brow collected
in the middle of her head
as he faced her. She barely looked
in his direction.
Water puddles at the drain.
He steps under the trickling tap.
Lukewarm spray wets his threaded cheek,
runs over each stud.
His eyelets upturned accept the shower.
No. She never recognized him,
even as he peered into her face,
even after he signed his credit card receipt.

FINDING MY FACE IN CARNIVAL

for Mosco

Remember we danced in La Avenida Chapultepec?
A dragonfly, a sorceress, and a mermaid wrapped
their dangly arms over stone statues like lovers.

Los Bomberitos strummed another tale of a man
tormented by a woman's eyes. Heels of men in drag
clicked over cobblestone. Gleaming under our sandals

like broken glass, the fallen purple jacaranda lay dying.
Every moving body was reticence disguised in new skin.
My spaghetti legs wobbled through the beats.

We palmed out *Dos Gardenias* under a crooked moon.
An old woman dressed in a child's bonnet cupped my head
in her hands and kissed me on the mouth.

Didn't we consider taking her home? I remember
our pause. Wasn't it you who plastered the cathedral walls
with glitter as strangers paired up and tumbled into new bars?

I remember our laughter stunted by a woman
costumed as a black-faced savage, how she monkey-walked
past us: her bone-bound hair, her septum ring,

and her loincloth all prancing to the tambor.
Didn't we fly into the heavy crowd of dogmen
and princesses? I clung to your arms, our clown faces

melting in the heat. You tapped a rhythm on my knees. I tried whispering
a new song. I was holding shame in the roof of my mouth.
We sweated through our costumes
and we cringed at our dirt-blackened feet.

LA BASE

la · bah'-say\: 1. The base or receiver of an aerial
power move. After one's opponent has already
jumped, la base must remain in place in order to
accept the blow, otherwise, la base risks injuries
to their opponent and/or one's self.

LA BASE

A few seconds until the end and I am hunched and breathless, an aching ball of body
kneeling center ring. The arena is all sneers and whistles while the other guy

scales ropes. With each of his steps, the turnbuckles' creaking warns me
to untangle my legs, to get up and steady my frame. I know

the only thing to do is wait. His arms will come down in an Axe
or maybe a Suicide Bomb. It doesn't matter the move,

he will somersault all his weight onto me, and I will shape
his descent. A flight must have a place to land,

two sore arms to catch and cradle him, another body
to fall into. When he hurtles through the air

and everything rushes past his mask,
I am the hinge, his net.

LEARNING TO ROLL OUR TONGUES, DETROIT 1986

Ms. Álvarez flips up a flash card and shows us a faded
red sphere. Two leaves cling to its stem. *Manzana*, apple.
All together, we say it. She nods, smiles. We sit
cross-legged, her rug with a map of the world frayed
under us. Our upturned eyes set on her pictures,
we wrap our brown lips over her florid sounds,
flicking the fruit off our tongues.

Oso, bear. No breakfast before school, our mothers
have sent us to repeat Spanish words. We suck
the sugary heads of animal crackers for midday snack.
The small cookie bodies softening in our mouths.
Some of us sneak an extra cookie bag. I've stuffed mine
in my pocket for later. One time Lawrence
choked from trying to swallow a lion whole.

The word *plátano*, banana, is easy on our teeth.
Two blocks away, a man knocks a woman to the ground.
Libro, book. The man is one of our fathers. *Cerdo*, pig.
His dry hands tighten around her throat. *Mariposa*, butterfly.
We mimic our teacher's pitch, curl the *p* out like a pout.

Gato, cat. We are anchored
to the rug's blue-red-green. *Azul. Rojo. Verde.*
He hits her again. Her knees scrape pavement.
España, Angola, Japón. I trace my fingers
over each country's translated name, imagine
the sounds at each border. She tries to escape.
No one stops his hitting. *Pájaro*, bird.
A robin stares sideways from our teacher's card.
It does not sing. It does not know trees,
nor nesting, nor migration.

ODE TO THE TONGUE

Click. Twist. Flutter. Once again
you stick a tepid towel sound in my mouth.
We are in a café, in a hotel, in a store
trying to order coffee or cookies and there you go.

The long *u* of you in my lap. I am a fractured
figurine. Language is made of spackled sounds
flitting past my eyes. We play naming games,
guess each mouth-shaped word made soft in their lips.

What you call imitation is a clanging arrest, a sour
misuse of the throat. I trip over syllables. I feel
sweat trickle between my breasts, let these
faraway words lie like fuzz on my teeth. Tongue,

have you noticed how troubled you have become?
I cannot maneuver conversation without you slipping
out of place. You twist around like a trapped bull.
I have tried to force you out of your silent ending.

We are native to people who can't stop speaking
foreign languages. There is no space for timidness,
tongue. Loop into a long word like *lung*. Lay
the lengthy trills on the backside of *paladar*.

At some tables, tongue and language
are the same. Don't bother translating decorum.
Each country sets, with its own formal address
and common clatter, a shock on the mouth.

In this mouth let's send a curled *g* galloping
across some desert with the *r*'s rolling ribbon heart.

GREAT MATCH

You'd think to yourself, "Take it easy. I am giving you my body." Of course you don't say that. You suck it up.—REY MYSTERIO

After the match say, *Thank you*
or *Nice work out there*, or *My God!*
Where'd you get those moves?

Don't lose your balance.
Don't topple. Gather your body
like a sack of cramped muscle and bones.

Though your arms drag like a ton
of ground meat, keep your fists
extended through the air.

Soft punch the others, wiggle
a two or three step dance
as if you'd just sprung

into the ring. Don't talk
about your knee's cartilage
or that you are afraid

of the unraveling sounds crackling
through your shoulders
each time you springboard

from the third rope.
Even if your neck opens
and your head hangs
by fibrous threads
say, *Thank you. Great match.*

NARCISSUS ON EL SANTO

Gum rot grinning
under holy eyelashes,
you endless land of muscle
capped by a seductive pinky toe.

You lean into your own face.
You hide callused
nipples and cauliflowered earlobes.
Stretched tendon, cramped
thigh, you're a strained awakening,
an awkward rise,
a collection of limbs at dawn.

You star in movies dragging
through days in tight skin, gazing
into half-full glasses. You don't like contact
with others' hands? You don't speak much,
do you? You think you are well,
cursed river man?

Your muscles will not cure you.
You wipe and dig cavities.
You chew mouth open
showing off all of you,
you slurp and smack, you limp
and shift. You'll ache.
You'll pop. You'll crack.
This is what happens to the botched
tongue, the tender fist.
The body unfolds
its murmuring heart
and slipped disk.

Admit it. Your internal bleed,
your burned back and scarred chin,
you break.

LOS EXÓTICOS

\los · ek-so'-tee-cos\: 1. A male wrestler who appropriates female characteristics into their wrestling persona.
2. A drag queen. Although an exótico may not be homosexual, he will often rattle a macho wrestler by flirting and making sexual advances during a match.

NEGRITA

\nə`grēta\: *f. n.* 1. A woman with dark skin: AS IN *If the Spanish girl is blanquita, and the Indian girl is morena, then you are definitely negrita;* AS IN *Although the baby was born negrita, she is still very pretty;* AS IN *We can always tell a negrita from her knuckles, curly hair, and gums;* AS IN *She has a nice figure and long hair despite being negrita.* 2. Term of endearment for a black woman: AS IN *Ay, negrita! Oh, mi negrita bonita!* 3. The diminutive of black: AS IN *Not that girl, the one who is slightly more negrita.* 4. A young black girl: AS IN *I saw las negritas leave for school every day;* AS IN *This is a school for negritas only.* 5. Bold or dark lettering: AS IN *La negrita always stands out on the white page; Never type in negrita, it offends.* 6. A golliwog: AS IN *Why is that negrita in my house?; Who invited the negrita?; My little girl does not play with the negrita; Surely someone else likes the negrita.* 7. Black coffee. 8. An Italian candy: AS IN *I held her in my mouth.* She said, Devour me. *I kept licking.* My sweet Negrita, *she repeated.* My sweet negrita, open your mouth.

MAMA SNAPS. I SALSA.

Esa negrita tiene su tumba'o
y cuando la gente la va mirando
ella baila de la'o
también apreta'o, apreta'o, apreta'o

—CELIA CRUZ

Every Thursday this band pumps
La Mutualista with a clave's core clink
so I trek a mile through downtown's dim
stone streets because in Guadalajara
the Cubans bring the best dancers
and I am choosy with men's hands.
The cantina's dance floor fills with tilts
and turns. Congas, trombones, and singers
climb up and down their solos. Keys
shaped from the pianist's fingers form
a forged parentage at my waist.
Here I am La Negra—not Gringa.
I tiptoe in high-tops while American girls
in new studio pumps stumble over
un-dos-tres. A sweaty palm guides me
as my lopsided paisanos collide
on awkward legs. My hips carve boundaries
into the hard floor. The bandleader winks
before he sings about a dark woman he loves
and how sad his home will be if she leaves.
Past the rope-fenced dance floor a Frenchman
pulls his Haitian wife close and they swing
in their tight circle through the band's last bang.
We are all migrants: our heads' subtle swish;
our kicks' slight slant. My dance partner asks
again and again, *¿Pero tú? ¿De donde eres?*

Back home my mother's radio is probably cranking
Marvin Gaye dedications or Luther Vandross apologies.
As she snaps on beat to each doo-wop
she remembers a dance hall man
who praised the dip in her waistband
and doubted Detroit fumes and motors
manufactured her worldly strut.
Salsa. Bachata. Chicago Step. I take on
each ritual dance. Adapting is a stomp
and blended spin. Here, I become
a camouflage of rolling *R*'s.

CASTAS

after Robert Colescott, Lightening Lipstick

1. Mulatto

Face it. You are too dark
for a hot pink dress.
Round nose, round belly,
round face—your dark face,
your lump-distorted face,
your two-toned face.
Two shades away
from doomed.
Too much history found
under your skin.
Face it. Buckled bloodline child
where so much blood
leads to lineage in that face.
A not so fresh or pure
or white like smoke. Face it.

2. Mestizo

In a dance hall
with my mouth,
I grabbed ahold
of a man
by his lips.
Sucked his saliva
down my throat.
I was two-stepping.
He said *Dance pretty girl*.
We were dancing—
I moved my hips.

He moved his.
We sang with the band
about a woman
with too many men
to think about just one.
He stepped to the right
and I went left.
It was nice. We were
a song. It was a duet
traveling up my spine
into a maybe,
but when I put my hand in his,
the deep ridges of his knuckles
were too dark and craggy.
Ridges I could not conquer.
I had to let him go.

3. *Torna atrás*

Who told you to traipse
down Fifth Ave. and not come back?
Everybody has a hinting of color
laid in the small of their back,
some black grandmother
tucked in their closet
and an Irish one, and a French one,
and I got some German
somewhere back there.
We all have a tangle of lines,
a dying stock throating out
a guttural slave song.
But, child, you've always had
my lips, my inverted hair.
You have my naked ass.

4. Tente en el aire

"Pero soy latina."
 "¡Ay, Negrita! No te hagas, ¿eh?"

5. Lobo

I got these six men
with six stories
trying to climb up my legs.
One says he likes how my sideburns
curl off my cheeks.
The other says he
likes 'em light skinned.
One thinks it's best
we stay in my neighborhood
lest we run into his family.
I prefer the man
who thinks our thighs
look like coconut water
and milk colliding and running
all over the sheets.

6. No te entiendo

Clip. Clip Clip. Clip
the nose. Clip the lips.
Clip belly. Clip hips.
Clip pigment. Clip. Clip.
Clip fingernail moons. Clip eyes.
Clip dreads. Clip afro. Clip
finger waves. Clip extensions.
Clip weave. Clip the batik.
The kente. The adinkra.
Clip. Clip. Clip. Clip buttocks.

Clip brown teat. Clip. Clip tongue.
Clip Boricua. Clip Yanga. Clip
the Quechua. Clip more
of the tongue. Clip more
of the tongue. Clip. Clip. Clip
more of the tongue. Clip. Clip. Clip.
Clip brown hands. Clip brown eyes.
Clip brown thighs. Clip. Clip. Clip.
Clip blood. Clip blood. Clip blood.

AMANUENSIS

Dearly beloved Brethren and Fellow Citizens,
My Lords and Gentlemen,
the following is an original account.

What I say and swear to you, reader,
is no lie. I know the wilted sound
my tongue makes trying on the suit
of a new country.
Each vendor or basket woman
will ask my neck to bend
and bend until it forgets its origin.
I know how misery fills a rented room.

In the month of May, 2005, I had the honor of meeting
a black woman born in the United States but whose
travels had brought her to reach four continents.
She had seen more foreign land than of her own country.

I landed in Paris, in Paraguay,
in Joburg carved up and divided.
Parts of me stood at the border
of history and others lay
in the land of commerce.

On this occasion she narrated to me
of her life and in this publication
she chooses to write her own narrative.

Another me ambled
through another unfamiliar town.
Coins spilled from my accent.
I had not come to overturn history's
rotten bricks. No part of me
was a mob-named fugitive.

You will find she is among the humblest of her race

There was an ugly happiness
to my arrival.
My body had grown pungent in travel.
I smelled of planes and buses
and me, moist and it was sweet.

and her adventures most telling

A fever rattled in my skin.
I farmed an Atlantic beach
for the flexed muscles of boys.

*and survival. I believe, you reader,
will find her and her cause compelling.*

How pale their upturned lips,
how they matched a moon sky.
How their mothers winced
at the thought, and
called the space between my legs
terror.

For her story is one of struggle.

Did I say *Save me*?

I slathered sunscreen
on my belly.

I was neither down nor out.

THE ART OF SPIRIT SUBMISSION: AN ARS POETICA

after Renée Stout, New Orleans, 2008–2010

What divinity's piecemeal
    is holy
unholy   and undone
I once saw a man—
    a mounting
He danced in circles
    reared his head
trembling
    and golden
and gone
I've seen a spirit
    ride a man
for four red hours
of a Chicago night
in a murky basement
Yemonja lit him up
took his body
tied her dress around his hips
feasted through his mouth
    I take the rouged
chard root,
    hold its leafy hands
under my floorboards
I dare not ask
    I sweep plantain
with smoke
I dare not beg
    a worship song
the whole of occupancy
    is to submit

give the body up into hallelujahs
I am—
    derailed / effaced
    seized
I want to use my words
                  —up and shaken
To be moun—
    to be stripped
I am gone, unraveled
    and reassembled
this muddy vessel business
             is to un-
    wind
turn over like lace tied fibers
    to attempt
to maintain my name
    is not veneration
the urgency of chant and drum
    grips me
I flick the heavy words
    as if the sacred, the not so sacred
and the things that fall apart
    under the slightest light
ring me
I cannot be taken
    unless I let them come

LUCHA DE APUESTA

\loo'-chah · day· ah-poo-ess'-tah\: A wager or a betting fight; putting one's mask or hair on the line to settle a feud. A luchador(a) who loses must remove their mask. If they have already lost their mask, their head will be shaved immediately.

HOW NOT TO LOSE THE MASK:
LUCHA DE APUESTA

for Perro Aguayo Jr. (1979–2015)

The bet was mask
for mask. This loser risked
his hair. Now
the winning fighter wields
the winning razor
in his right hand. A tuft
of the sorry sap's locks
in his left. I'll bet
my money for your car.
His house for your
dressing room.
She who loses
will work as a servant
for the champion.
Drowning
for electric shock.
And when there is nothing
on the line, everything is on the line.
His elbow's last lace of cartilage
will give. One too many hits
might shatter her knee.
Most lucky wrestlers
will lose mobility in two places,
while the unlucky—
three broken vertebrae,
his last breath
slipping from his chest.
If I don't take you down
you win my wife,
or my first son,
my blood, my ears, air.

But you will lose memories:
your grandmother's face,
how to tie a knot,
the digits of your address.
How to win at risking?
What do we win?
A wandering walk
in a new suburb
naming all familiar
and foggy things.

HOW NOT TO LOSE THE MASK: TAKE DOWN THE MAN WHO GRABS YOUR CROTCH WHILE ON YOUR WAY TO CHURCH

When bells swing through their soft
devotional clang, when you are near

and can recognize pastel flowers
ruffled in a girl's church dress,

you will pass the stubby man—
your opponent. You might take him

for another worshipper, or merely
a drowsy morning pedestrian.

When he reaches his thick arm
towards you, you might not realize

where he is aiming. You might not understand
until he seizes you, until you've already caught

his dirty fat hand, and spun the both of you so that now
you face each other. You might blurt out

¡Hijo de tu puta madre! and *¡Pendejo!* and *¡Mierda!*
Summon every curse you can remember.

You might be too far for any priest to notice
your assault. Make the most of this match. Twist his arm

at the wrist. If you can, an elbow bend.
The struggle might feel like a lifetime,

but let's face it, your grip has never held on long.
So keep cursing. Do not stutter. See

how his startled eyes roll open.
Call his foul. Repeat *¡Pinche*

cabrón! When he loosens your grip
and takes off running, chase him.

That's allowed. You might even follow him for blocks.
Even if you stay planted in your tiny square of sidewalk,

keep cursing. Call him *¡Pendejo!* again.

THE FIRST GUY: NO REVERENCE, NO PRAISE, NO CALLING UPON

Bored with their playground hummingbirds
and lizards, Hurakan and some other gods
dropped to their knees and shoved their hands

in mud. A constellation of fingers
and feathers molding calf and lips,
spackling sand and water,

as if I were a mud pie or a sandcastle.
They wanted someone to praise them,
to fetch them a feast, but I was born

coughing up brown puddles, my knees fell to pieces.
Clay-colored robins viewed the creators from treetops.
Gucumatz slapped on my ears. The sound was slosh and gurgle.

My head didn't turn. My torso was twisted. My mouth came to pieces
at my jaw. *More dirt!* shouted mother Xpiyacoc, packing soft flesh
onto my crumbling arms, but without a sun or heat to dry me,

I was a putty sculpture abandoned for sticks. Later
they pulled up the neighbor's corn. Me? I was tossed
onto the riverbank. I was a failed psalm,

waiting for another creator
to work the living out of me.

VASCONCELOS MEETS SKIP GATES

His wide lens pans over my coral town.
He combs through my fingernails,
takes his cleaver to my nose,
If it looks like a duck . . .

He knows the dark black
under my eyelid, tucked
in a shadow of breast.
Skip leans towards the camera,

And acts like a duck . . .
He is waddling past my lace
rebozos hanging on my iron gate
past my glass-bead necklaces,
he is separating diphthongs

from coffee, yucca from tobacco. *Traditionally . . .*
Though I'm a blend between
checkers and thick mustaches,
he is finding the drops,
my paw and fur.

He will not admit mine is not
a story that starts nor ends
at this coastal table.
Skip grunts for his cane,
If this were the U.S. . . .
and we all become pretty
darkened things.

I want to seize his tongue,
pull the Celtic hairs from his beard,
show him that he too has
a closet-hidden grandmother.

But in his books, in his chronicle
I am mulatto, I am zambo, I am lobo,

so I give in. Engulfed by the show,
I strum strum strum the tight
strings of my guitar.
I say it. *Sí, señor. Soy Negro.*

A woman scoops a pinch of green dal and rice.
What has she done with her hair? Has she done this
on purpose? She throws the scoop on her tongue.
I like the other one they sent, says the weaver
without looking up from her loom. *She was bright*
and had such white teeth. Too dark for sacrifice,
says the Brahmin. A Newar snorts, hacks
and spits at my feet. *Send us a new one.*
And if we play music? says the poet. *She may dance*
like Ganesha. And they all keep guessing,
A student? How old? American? But where is she from?
Where is her father?

BUT IT'S NOT REAL. IT'S ALL FOR SHOW.

Faking it? I've taken my teeth
to a man's brow, thrashed my boot
into a fallen fighter.

I forge no fake calluses.
Two molars, a fractured rib,
a sprained finger in '99—

I mastered the skill of convincing
the body to resist the performance
of injury. Temple to ankle,

I risk backbreaking points
of each grating joint. I've laid my legs
under my opponents' whims.

Every man controls planned pain
through reversal-takedown-pin,
but when a doctor pulled my torn ligament

three inches up my thigh
to attach it back to bone,
I couldn't coax my stunted walk

into something smooth or cool.
There is no pretending that my steps
through the black curtain aren't vexed

by the tricky pull and snap in my back.
The smoke coiling up my booted legs
is so real. My tight neck so much more.

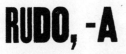

RUDO, -A

roo'-doh -ah\: 1. A brutal brawler. 2. Rule breaker.
3. A cheater. Also known as a heel, or a hooligan.
In lucha libre, a fan of los rudos will display allegiance
by wearing a single black glove.

RUDO

As a kid, you ever rinse your hands in another boy's spit?
Ever stay out, running corners past 3 a.m.,

or held a boy's head on a railroad track?
Or were you a "brains not fist" type,

the one whose scrawny neck looked like
a drowned bird's swallowed by an ocean

of oversized dress shirts? Rudo,
I bet a younger you kept your elbows clean.

I bet you never busted out a car window
nor threw rocks off an overpass.

You seem like the type that never even played
chicken. What made you slip the black leather glove

of cheater, so snug on your hand? Who gave you away
to weights and masks? When I was thirteen, I ran

with neighborhood boys. We discovered
how dry ice and water trapped in a plastic bottle

pressurizes to a bomb. We filled empty two-liters,
twisted the plastic caps tight, and ran.

Tiny explosions boomed up and down our block
until DuJuan held on to the tiny weapon too long.

Our street filled with the blast and crash
of a boy crouched and wailing. But like you,

I am a runner. I kept away. I let adults handle his hand.
From my porch I watched the clatter of plastic shrapnel

shred his thumb, his tearless stumble and silent stand.
And you are a runner—a groin-kicking, face-biting

runner. We are always running, learning how to scam
the rules, running from corner to corner, hiding blades

close to our tights. What was it for you? Was it the night your father
leaned into your face, his Tecate sweating in his palm?

He called you *little mariposa*, his sweet little shit.
Or was it the boys who beat you until your face
was lumpy as a ripe avocado? What made you

desire to crack your hands on skulls? What turned you
towards tightening your arms around a man's neck,

pressing hard till he taps out?
DuJuan's mangled, black hand kept me

from grabbing another bottle. I've taken to tighter
moves, ones that don't make me think of such risks.

CALL THE MATCH

When he pins your shoulders to the mat,
you'll use all your limbs to throw his hold,

whip your legs around his torso. Scissor him down.
The crowd might cheer, they might heckle.

Cigarette smoke will curl into the spotlights,
and the small room will feel like your guaranteed win.

None of this matters. You're supposed to lose.
After you backbend his body, you will take a headbutt.

He will launch you from the ring into the stands.
You will fall, flat-faced. Your twisted body

will feel its knotted ache. Make it look good.
Let him win. Refuse to get up. Listen

for the low hiss of breath escaping your chest.
It will feel like a tornado churning between your ribs.

In a different fight, in a different city, in a different ring,
you will make another man plead through the calls,

but tonight you'll taste salt, you'll taste the metal in your own
bloody lip. When he slams your forehead into a bleacher, lie there

openmouthed, shocked even, as if this is not the plan. Fold
to pain. Submit to the job. Fall. A boy in the second row

will launch potato chips into your face. A wrinkled woman
might call you coward. Though they know your body,

the arena, and their seat in your world are a false framework,
each fanatic spectator will swarm the ring demanding

you perform the calls. The crowd will hate you.
The crowd will love the choreography of the takedown.

The crowd will go home satisfied.

In each sentence I turn
over what I mean to say,
but my words are undercut
by my body. I say *I'm here, lover.*
I love. I ... I ... I ...

amigo   mágico   amor
For you I translate a dream:
buganvilla   *flor*   tumbling
from my elbows and knees.

I am always undoing the language
of my body.
My arms, my hair say
Black.   Dark.   English only.

You grab the sounds in my fingers.
You hang a flat fish
from my teeth.
       No.
These are our words
rendered in our kitchen,
on our balcony at night.

I say *kin.*
You see skin. We are a lake
of *How do I say* and *Si sabes lo que es.*

Then my body
says *no   no   no   no*
la   la   la   la
This assemblage of words and body
tightens into bad blood. Still,

I mouth them,
a litany of words
luz   almohada   labios

They shadow windows, dwell
in the spacious folds
of our bed linen.

I've seen you stumble over
my warped words.

You rub them, gently,
between two fingers.

Some nights
while night birds cackle
in the streets, when you think
sleep has wrapped my head
in its heavy blanket
I see you place my *Oh*
on your tongue.

GUADALAJARA IN THE FORM OF LITANY
(2001–2005)

after Gabrielle Calvocoressi

Fire seared through La Primavera and home kept calling.
My country declared war and home kept calling.
The corn husks wilted and home kept calling.

The city was choking and home kept calling.
The sun bleached my rooftop laundry and home kept calling.
I sipped Fanta with Herradura and home kept calling.

My president bragged about foreign oil and home kept calling.
Quinceañeras filled downtown squares. I thought of home. I didn't call.
Smoke dirtied the air and home kept calling.

Children donned surgical masks in school and home kept calling.
Propane vendors dragged through the streets and home kept calling.
The oven fireballed through my kitchen and home kept calling.

The month I came home Guadalajara kept calling.
The soldiers found Saddam and home kept calling.
Mother said, *I don't need you. Go back.* Home kept calling.

Men sang serenades and home kept calling.
My asthma flared and home kept calling.
Las Chivas won Mexico and home kept calling.

My eyelashes were singed and home kept calling.
Mother's house was foreclosing and home kept calling.
I got lost in subtitles and home kept calling.

Pepper-limed jicama shimmered from street-food carts.
I called it home. I said just one more year.
Detroit was going black and blue from calling and calling.

Mother's legs were pinned to the couch and home kept calling.
The doctors said *surgery* and home kept calling.
The doctors said *degenerative* and *permanent damage*.

Mother's nerves were burning out and home kept calling.
I called home. *Don't fret*, Mother said.
Home will always be calling.

THE WARNING

for Ai

So many beautifully bloodied sounds
tucked under my chin, breaking
under pressurized note. I've made it

through the night working lines into a damp thigh,
a stalled truck, a woman humming
into her husband's ear. Without occasion

or motive, I've buried voices. I've studied
the slow motion of carving
breast meat. I shadow the butcher's

cut. I feel my face's open grin
when I sharpen my shears.
The baritone of a bruised man's

chuckle rattles my lungs. A child's starlike
hand reaches across my belly. I have to yank
them out. I had never heard wanting

strapped to a boy's wrists
until I tied him down, made him sing.
I'm a borrower of voice boxes, a surgeon

of tongues. I am warning you: you ought to stop
loving me; you ought not lay your story
on my counter; you ought to be careful

before I take you up by your throat,
before you find yourself barefoot
in my kitchen, mute and panting.

Eufrosina, has your son run off again?
He's cracked the cookie jar. He's turned over
the wash. He's taken a shit on someone's table

again. Yolanda, your blue-black child
used to be so good, until he heard
no black angels get into heaven. You told him

to copy Cleopatra, to soak
his body in milk. You made him break
all the delicate porcelain. You made him

a runaway. Memín, where have you gone?
In what dark face are you hiding? I know
schoolboys hanker after your weekend wild,

high-five your kicks and runs, but ban you
from class. Their fair girls whip plain ponytails
in your face. This is no home for shoeshine boys.

But where are you? Was that you in Sambo's
Soul Food dining with Speedy Gonzales? Wasn't that you
cracking into a bucket of Sebastian's ripple crab legs,

butter running the curve of your chubby chin?
Oh Memo, you dirty little boy with deformed
little hands and cheeks drawn molasses thick. I know I saw

your bulging eyes in Mexico City, your monkey ears
in a café in Santo Domingo. In New York your body,
a splayed reprint, is boxed and stamped,

on candy wrappers. Hog-tied and gagged
in Accra, you lay, large lips
zipped. You're an inerasable grin,
rooted in every street of us.

"ESTÁN HACIENDO TRABAJOS QUE NI SIQUIERA LOS NEGROS QUIEREN HACER"

—President Vicente Fox, Mexico

1.

¡Ay diós! We are in the computer lab when I hear it.
A voice purr from a mouth, stain the air. I hear it
whine over our keyboards like a sad mosquito

come too late in the season. *¡Ay diós!*
It is grading time and we teachers crowd
into the school's only lab the way teachers

with grading must. *Me tienes aquí trabajando*
We all have a load. We all face our computers
and pick at our students' labor.

We check boxes and the room stays so quiet until
¡Ay diós! Me tienes aquí trabajando como un negro.
Her sigh and groan. I hear it.

Me tienes aquí trabajando como un Negro.
Others hear it, *me tienes aquí trabajando.*
I don't have to look up to see who said it.

I never have to look to see who's saying.
Como un Negro I am always. *Como un Negro*
the voice crawls to me. *Como un negro trabajando.*

2.

Ay Nandi, no seas así. Aquí en México no hay racismo porque no hay negros.

78

3.

You have me working like a slave.
You got me working like a nigger.
Me tienes trabajando como un Negro.

Never in my cotton-pickin' years.
You alligator bait, you fortune cookie,
you Indian giver. How to let the tongue
do its work down my leather-skinned back?
What offense was not meant, is dealt

is taken. Dig into the weighty work song:
dirt, laundry, landscaping. Widen
a crater for all the sounds:
wetback-gypsy-coon-coolie.
Slack limp words, pitch them
down the center *O*
of job. Let the work fall in.

TÉCNICO, -A

tec'-nee-co-ah\: 1. A technical fighter; a fighter who follows the rules. 2. A craftsman. Also known as "face" or "baby face." In lucha libre los técnicos are almost always the fan favorites.

TAMED

I want the tongue to earn its place
on the clavicle. And the palm

to form the shape of pelvis, of forearm,
of shin. I want the body to disappear

under tremble. And the heart
with its golden petals? If bone
were infrangible, and the eyes

not such delicate recorders—
but no. I want the bite, and the raking

nail. Body, can't you imagine
the arresting scale, the spine's

tense arch? I fight
your hum, your perpetual want.
But the frame, but all my cavities

unplumbed and quivering.

LOSING THE MASK

1. El Luchador

When the laces loosened and gave,
a cool air and calm hit my face. The ring's gasp
clogged my ears. Not silent. Not chaos.
It was as if I'd mangled my hand on a job. I lost
my face, placed my creased grin
into my audience's palms. Losing my mask
was like having my torso ripped out. Then
I offered it still trembling to the winner.
My face, my exposed veins pumping
over my forehead. I was no lazy factory worker
losing my thumb under a negligent power saw.
Not a chef cutting too quickly at a raw carrot.
I lost. I put on a good face—
my face. I dragged the rest of my body
through the arena, through warm back halls,
to my locker. Pulled my arms into my shirt,
and tugged at the buckle of my belt. I dressed
my body in plain clothes. I broke.

2. La Máscara

Before I let go, before they part me open,
before they pull you, headfirst, out of me,
and hand me over to a man
who will take me and hang me,
before I become a sparkling medallion,
a memory, a relic of slaughter,
you have got to loosen all the strings.
You will always have hair,
boots, and tape. In a year

you can go to a mall or grocery store,
you can walk through the dust
of a market and everyone will know
the bottom lip and callused forehead
I have kept so long inside. M'hijo,
before I let go of your face,
someone will have to rip me apart.

"How Not to Lose the Mask: Mil Máscaras Showers after a Match" and "Great Match": The Rey Mysterio quotations that appear in the epigraphs are taken from Jeremy Roberts, *Rey Mysterio: Behind the Mask* (New York: Gallery Books, 2010).

"Castas": A reference to the "castas," categorizations conceived by the Spanish colonizers to identify the new "races" that resulted from racial mixing in Latin America. Each section of the poem begins with a term the Spanish applied to a population. *Torna atrás* ("jump backward"), *tente en el aire* ("floating midair"), and *no te entiendo* ("I don't undertand you") are among the unofficial classifications that emerged. While legal *casta* designations were formally abolished when Mexico gained independence in 1821, terms such as *moreno, mestizo*, and *mulato* are still used to refer to color and racial mixture.

"Vasconcelos Meets Skip Gates": José Vasconcelos was a Mexican writer and philosopher who outlined a theory of the "cosmic race" that identifies mestizo blood as the most sophisticated example of civilization. Henry Louis Gates Jr. (Skip Gates) is a scholar and critic of African American culture who specializes in the history of African influence on the world.

"Guadalajara in the Form of Litany (2001–2005)": The poem is after Gabrielle Calvocoressi's "Late Twentieth Century in the Form of Litany."

"Memín Pinguín": Memín Pinguín is a popular pickaninny-like character created by Yolanda Vargas Dulché in the early 1940s. He and his mother, Eufrosina, were Cuban immigrants living in Mexico. In 2005 the Mexican postal service issued a series of commemorative stamps featuring the character.

The title is a quotation from former president of Mexico Vicente Fox, said when reflecting on the plight of Mexican immigrants in the United States. It roughly translates, "They are doing the work that even the blacks don't want to do." *Me tienes aquí trabajando como un Negro* is a common saying that, in the U.S. context, means "You have me working like a slave."

"Tamed": The lines "And the heart / with its golden petals" are adapted with slight variations from Federico García Lorca's poem "Ghazal of the Terrifying Presence."

Thank you to the editors and staff of the following publications in which the following poems first appeared:

Journals

Callaloo: "Postcards, A Self-Portrait"

Chиricú Journal: Latina/o Literatures, Arts and Cultures: "Uncle Rod Watches Man on Fire," "Narcissus on El Santo"

Crab Orchard Review: "Detroit, Llorona, My Heart, My City," "Losing Between Manholes and Myths," "The Warning"

Green Mountains Review Online: "On Becoming a Fan," "The Idol's Mask," "I Dream I Am a Doña Dreaming of Lucha"

Muzzle Magazine: "How Not to Lose the Mask: Mil Mascaras Showers after a Match"

Southern Indiana Review: "La Base" and "Call the Match"

Spoon River Poetry Review: "Tamed"

Sycamore Review: "Memín Pinguín"

Books

"On Coming Home to Teach" previously appeared in *American Family: A Syndrome; Poems* (Georgetown, Ky.: Finishing Line Press, 2018). Copyright © 2018 by Nandi Comer. Reprinted with the permission of The Permissions Company, LLC, on behalf of Finishing Line Press, www. finishinglinepress.com.

"Learning to Roll Our Tongues" previously appeared in Anna Clark, ed., *A Detroit Anthology* ([Cleveland, Ohio]: Rust Belt Chic Press, 2014).

"¡Sangre! ¡Sangre! ¡Sangre!" previously appeared in Natalie Diaz, ed., *Bodies Built for Game: The Prairie Schooner Anthology of Contemporary Sports Writing* (Lincoln: University of Nebraska Press, 2019).

Illustrations by Miguel Valverde

COVER: *Lady Poison* (2019; acrylic on canvas)

PAGE 4: *Mortal hacia atrás* (2018; acrylic and polymer)